To the Top

LEVEL 1

/d/o/

DECODABLES

BY jump!

Teaching Tips

Pink Level 1

This book focuses on the phonemes **/d/o/**.

Before Reading

- Discuss the title. Ask readers what they think the book will be about.
- Sound out the words on page 3 together.

Read the Book

- Ask readers to use a finger to follow along with each word as it is read.
- Encourage readers to break down unfamiliar words into units of sound. Then, ask them to string the sounds together to create the words.
- Urge readers to point out when the focused phonics phonemes appear in the text.

After Reading

- Encourage children to reread the book independently or with a friend.
- Ask simple questions about the text to check for understanding. Have them find the pages that have the answers to your questions.

North American adaptations © 2024 Jump!
5357 Penn Avenue South
Minneapolis, MN 55419
www.jumplibrary.com

Decodables by Jump! are published by Jump! Library.

Library of Congress Cataloging-in-Publication Data is available at www.loc.gov or upon request from the publisher.

ISBN: 979-8-88996-777-4 (hardcover)
ISBN: 979-8-88996-778-1 (paperback)
ISBN: 979-8-88996-779-8 (ebook)

Photo Credits

Images are courtesy of Shutterstock.com. With thanks to Getty Images, Thinkstock Photo and iStockphoto. Cover – Pixel-Shot. 4–5 – Gyorgy Barna. 6–7 – Luciavonu, Piotr Wytrazek. 8–9 – Gyorgy Barna. 10–11 – Gyorgy Barna, Piotr Wytrazek. 15 – Shutterstock.

Can you find these words in the book?

dad

dip

pot

top

Go up, Dad!

To the top, Dad.

Dip it in a pot.

Dip, dip, dip.

Go, Dad!

Dad is at the top.

Dip, dip, dip.

Back to the top, Dad.

Can you say these sounds and draw them with your finger?

Using the Letter Bank, trace the missing letter into each word.

__op

__ad

p__t

d__p

Letter Bank

d o t i

What other words do you know with the letters /d/ or /o/?

dot

mud

dig

doll

Practice reading the book again:

Go up, Dad!

To the top, Dad.

Dip it in a pot.

Dip, dip, dip.

Go, Dad!

Dad is at the top.

Dip, dip, dip.

Back to the top, Dad.